ALRESFORD

1900 *2000*

A CENTURY OF VILLAGE LIFE IN POSTCARDS AND PHOTOGRAPHS
by John Hedges

H. AND C. PUBLICATIONS

First published (c) 2000 by John M. Hedges
Alresford, Colchester, Essex, CO7 8DU

ISBN 0 9530633 5 6

British Library / Cataloguing in Publication Data
A catalogue record for this book is available from the British Library.

Typesetting and Reprographics by LazerType, Colchester

Printed and bound by Lavenham Press

Front Cover shows a tranquil scene of barges at rest in the Alresford Creek

To my wife Margaret, Graham and Sandra

Cover photograph courtesy Alresford Sand and Ballast Company
Back cover photograph courtesy Mr. Ivan Thompson

Contents

	Page
Alresford Postcard	1
Branch Line	2
Cattle Crossing	3
Iron Swing Bridge	4
Iron Swing Bridge	5
Reflections in the Creek	6
View from the Sand Works	7
Barges at Rest	8
Ford Cottage	9
Plumptons Farm	10
Seed Harvest	11
Windmill	12-13
Thorrington Tide Mill	14
Derelict Tide Mill	15
South Lodge	16
Lodge Farm	17
Lodge Farm	18
Rural Scene	19
Garden Produce	20-21
Lodge House	22
Alresford Hall	23
Matthew Martin	24-25
The Quarters House	26-27
Missing Constable Painting	28-29
Wivenhoe Park Painting	30
War Memorial, St. Peter's Church	31
St. Peter's Church	32-33
Church Wedding	34
Church Fire	35

	Page
St. Peter's Ruins	36
Robert Bray's Tomb	37
Alresford Rectory	38
Stained Glass Window	39
Pritchard Family Portrait	40
Alresford Mother's Union	41
The Cabin	42
Church Farm	43
Church School, 1846	44
Church School, 1913	45
School Group, 1900	46
School Group, 1909	47
School Group, 1921	48
School Group, 1935-38	49
School Group, 1956	50
Village Hall Committee	51
School Concert	52
Children's Outing	53
Alresford Optimists	54
Village Baby Show	55
Church Choir	56
Old Codgers Football Team	57
Alresford Eagles Football Team	58
Ladies Keep Fit Group	59
Alresford Joggers	60
Heather Cottage	61
1st. Alresford Guide Company	62
1st. Alresford Guide Company	63
Alresford Primary School	64

	Page
St. Andrews Church	65
Ford Lane Cottages	66
Meads Corner, Wivenhoe Road	67
Charabanc Outing, Wivenhoe Road	68
North Lodge	69
Children in Wivenhoe Road	70-71
Wivenhoe Road Forge	72
Fanmans Farm	73
Brook Farm	74
High Elms Farm	75
Alresford Café	76
Mr. Jim Bird	77
Alresford Bakery	78-79
Shopping Precinct	80-81
Rail Crossing Keeper	82
Alresford Station	83
Railway Station Staff	84
Park Farm Orchard	85
Cockaynes Farm	86-87
Pointer Inn	88-89
Coronation Ceremony	90
Wivenhoe Road	91
Bottle and Glass, Wivenhoe Road	92
Alresford Silver Band	93
Alresford Silver Band	94
Mr. Wilson Marriage	95
Alresford Grange	96-97
Map of Alresford	98

Acknowledgements

IAM greatly indebted to early contributors of the "Alresford Advertiser," and especially to the late Dudley White and Albert Carter for their fine research and contributions to the heritage of Alresford.

I wish to acknowledge my grateful and sincere thanks to the following people who have given up so much of their valuable time to discuss and provide me with so much intimate and historical information combined with the many enjoyable hours spent trying to bring names and faces together, or putting dates and places concerning a way of life in this village one hundred and fifty years ago.

Whilst many people have made valuable contributions to this book, I must also acknowledge the original photographers, artists and researchers who recorded the scenes and events many years ago, and without whose contribution it would not have been possible to have produced such a veritable record of Alresford's history.

I am therefore indebted to the following people who have made available their treasured family photographs and documentation to support the text in this book.

The following list of names is not in any particular order, they are however, all equally important to the outcome of this book: Alresford Advertiser, Eric Potter, *Ford Cottage;* Florrie Goodwin, *School Groups;* Paula Munson, *Guides & Church;* Jo Leeder, *Pilkington Family & Lodge Farm;* Robin and Mavis Grinsted, *Cockaynes, Fanmans & Brook Farm;* Percy Castle, *Pointer Inn;* Sir William and Lady Boulton, *Quarters House;* Derek and Ann Pentney, *Plumptons Farm;* National Maritime Museum, *Matthew Martin;* Michael Ennew, *Alresford Bakery;* Jenny Hughes, *Optomists;* Paul Brown, *Extracts from 'The Wivenhoe and Brightlingsea Railway;'* Tom Glover, *Thorrington Tide Mill;* Sonia Dean, Senior Curator of European Art, National Gallery of Victoria, Australia, *Constable's Painting;* Patrick Denney, *Local Historian;* Ray Milburn, *General support for this book;* Beryl Ridgers, *Alresford Colne Rangers;* Alan Green, *Alresford Colne Rangers;* Joan Alexander, *Alresford Café;* Dorothy Waller, *Lodge Farm;* Margaret Fitch, *Girl Guides;* Mabel Sallows, *Girl Guides;* Ken Jennings, *Silver Band;* Peter Sainty, *Heather Cottage;* Alresford Sand and Ballast Company, *Scenes at Alresford Creek;* David Greenacre, *Lodge Farm;* Pauline Hunt, *Railway Crossing;* Barry Neubronner, Penelopy Carter, and Sue Colebeck, *Various photographs;* Mrs. W. Thompson, *Sand and Ballast Company;* Essex County Standard, *Last Train and Alresford Silver Band;* Richard Shackle, *Local Studies, Colchester Library;* Colchester Museums Resources Centre, *Matthew Martin Portrait;* Elaine Wood, *Gladys Welham;* Barbara Byrne, *Gladys Welham;* David Craze, *Ford Lane Cottage;* Jack Hall, *Alresford Grange;* Ivy Randolph, *Checking Manuscript.*

Finally and by no means least, my extreme thanks go to David Clark who has supported me throughout and given me so much technical help, thank you Dave.

Whilst I have tried to mention everyone who contributed towards the writing of this book, names may have inadvertently been overlooked, if this has occurred, it is with great regret and in no way intentional.

Introduction

THE village of Alresford was so named from the Alders that grew by the Ford, according to a Gazetteer and Directory dated 1848 which states that: "Alresford is a pleasant village and parish on the eastern side of the vale of the river Colne 5.0 miles S.E. of Colchester, containing 289 souls and 1427 acres of land, watered by two rivulets which fall into a creek of the River Colne on the south side of the parish. The creek is fordable at low water.

Today, one could be forgiven for thinking that Alresford, once described as 'The Forgotton Village' by a local newspaper did not exist. This news heading was largely due to the fact that the village is partially hidden from public view by passing motorists on their way to either Colchester or the seaside resorts of Clacton on Sea, Frinton on Sea, or Walton on the Naze.

My purpose in compiling and writing of this book is to provide a permanent record of our village, also to ensure that ALRESFORD, which has a wealth of history and an excellent record of social events, does in fact exist and is not 'The Forgotton Village' as once described.

It is not my intention to display purely a collection of nostalgic, old and recent photographs with just a brief mention. What I hope to produce is a selection of postcards and photographs that with the aid of additional text have captured the imagination and atmosphere of 150 years ago between the manorial periods of the 19th century to more recent times.

I have arranged the book as a tour of Alresford commencing at the Wivenhoe Brightlingsea Railway Junction. Our journey will take us along the river Colne past the Victorian Iron Swing Bridge, and into the Alresford Creek, here we continue towards Thorrington Tide Mill before heading back past the Sand & Ballast works, so important to our village from an employment and environmental aspect. As we continue along Ford Lane, we pass the interesting and historical Alresford Manor estate incorporating the Quarters House. A map of Alresford can be seen on page 98 of this book for those readers who would like to follow the route of this tour.

The nearby ruins of St. Peter's Church clearly display the tragic remains of this once beautiful Saxon building sadly destroyed by fire in 1971.

Alresford has seen many changes over the years, none more so than in the 1960s when the village was transformed from a sleepy rural and agricultural village into a more populated commuter outpost with a population in excess of 3000 souls. A Post Office Directory of 1845 gave the Alresford population as 289 souls.

Whilst this book is almost totally devoted to the village of Alresford, it will be noticed that mention has been made of two neighbouring villages Wivenhoe and Thorrington. I make no apology for this inclusion as these villages are so relative to the photographs contained within this book'

As you turn these pages, I hope this compilation of pictures, combined with additional text, will reflect the many aspects of social and educational life in Alresford at the turn of the 20th century as well as in more recent times.

JOHN HEDGES

JUST a CARD from

ALRESFORD.

ALRESFORD POSTCARD

JUST a CARD from ALRESFORD was specifically designed for visitors as well as local residents, this card displays five delightful cameos of our village.

The postcard industry took off in 1894 with small cards measuring $4\frac{1}{2}$ x $3\frac{1}{2}$ referred to as Court Cards. Size further increased in 1895/1896. Postcards with divided backs for address and message came into being from 1902 and were similar to those of today.

Pictured top left to right are: The Alresford Swing Bridge and Railway Station. Pictured bottom left to right are: Corner shop, known as Meads / Jones Corner after their owners, and Boarded Cottages in Ford Lane, home to three families. Centre of postcard is an early view of St. Peter's Church.

Brightlingsea Branch flooded Sunday 23/11/03.

BRANCH LINE

This unique picture complete with caption taken in 1903 is really the start of our tour of Alresford. It shows the severely flooded area of the branch line beyond the Wivenhoe signal box through to Alresford, and on to Brightlingsea. Opened on 18th April 1866 as part of the 'Tendring Hundred Railway', this line was known locally as the "Oyster Creek Line" due to an oyster industry that once existed in Brightlingsea. Flooding was again to affect this line in 1904 threatening closure. The disastrous flooding of the East Coast in 1953 actually closed this line from January to December 1953.

Following the 'Beeching' rail cuts in the 1960s, this line was finally closed. The last train to run from Brightlingsea was in June 1964, five months later, gangers congregated to rip up the rails, wooden blocks and metal shoes and to rip out the heart, so it said at the time, of a whole community.

CATTLE CROSSING

In this peaceful scene thought to have been taken about 1885, a group of cattle are seen patiently waiting for the next train to pass before being escorted by the farmer across the railway line and into a nearby meadow. Alresford has long been an agricultural village. The spectacle of cattle roaming the fields and lanes was not uncommon until comparatively recent times. The grazing meadow beyond the gate probably belonged to the owners of Lodge Farm.

The iron swing bridge spanning the Alresford Creek and the small pilot-man's white hut can just be seen in the distance.

IRON SWING BRIDGE

The Iron Swing Bridge seen in this picture c.1905 was quite a talking point at the time. Built in 1845, it enabled the short length of railway line appropriately known as the 'Oyster Creek Line' because of an existing oyster industry, to link the small town of Wivenhoe with the coastal resort of Brightlingsea. This bridge when opened allowed barges to navigate the river up to Thorrington Mill and latterly to transport minerals extracted by the Alresford Sand and Ballast Company from a nearby timber jetty.

Notice a man standing on the bridge and the Edwardian lady in her crinoline dress standing in the extreme left hand corner of the picture.

IRON SWING BRIDGE

This nostalgic photograph shows one of the last passenger steam trains out of Brightlingsea crossing over the now-demolished iron swing bridge on its way to either Colchester or Brightlingsea.

The bridge was 430 feet in length and rested on sixteen large concrete pillars. When the centre span swung open through 90°, it rested, on two wooden piled piers rising from the riverbed. When the Bridge was used after the opening of the Branch Line, it allowed ships to pass through to Thorrington Tide Mill. In latter days the Bridge was opened to allow these ships to reach the Alresford Sand & Ballast Company's pier on the north side of the bridge. The Bridge was usually left open for shipping two hours before and after high tide, and only if a train was due. Originally, two Alresford men would row out to the centre of the Bridge to open or close it. Following the 'Beeching' rail cuts in the 1960s, the last train to cross this bridge from Brightlingsea was in June 1964.

Three years later, the Victorian Swing Bridge was dismantled leaving a huge gap between the Brightlingsea and Alresford shores.

REFLECTIONS IN THE CREEK

The Ford at Alresford Creek, now deserted except by holiday makers at weekends used to be quite a busy and industrial place with sailing barges going up on the tide to Thorrington Mill, whilst others unloaded slates or lime, or carried away cargoes of straw for the London stables.

This peaceful photograph shows a number of small pleasure craft resting at low tide just inside the Alresford creek from the river Colne. In the distance can be seen the banks of East Mersea generally known for its camping sites and nature reserves.

VIEW FROM THE SAND WORKS

This interesting picture gives an almost aerial view of the sand and ballast works in Alresford. A barge can be seen passing through the open swing bridge on its way to pick up a cargo of ballast or possibly products from the nearby tide mill.

Sand extracted from these works was conveyed in buckets suspended from an overhead gantry, this ran from the sandpits to barges anchored at a jetty below.

The Sand and Ballast Company, which began in 1930/1 by the Barrel family of Wivenhoe, has created much employment in the village of over many years. Pits that have served their useful purpose have been left alone allowing nature to transform them into natural habitats for wildlife as well as providing excellent fishing facilities for residents of Alresford.

BARGES AT REST

This tranquil picture, selected for the front cover of this book shows barges at rest alongside a timber built jetty. The jetty, such a familiar sight in Alresford today was originally built from timbers surplus to requirements in the building or extending of the Clacton pier.

Barges from London and other areas frequently called at this jetty to pick up supplies of sand and ballast that had been excavated from the nearby sandpits. It's interesting to note that aggregate from Alresford was used during the Second World War in the construction of some Suffolk airfields.

Note the gantry on the left of picture that conveyed the sand and ballast to the barges. Also seen in the background is the smugglers cottage, known locally as Ford Cottage.

FORD COTTAGE

Built around the 1650s, this timber built cottage located at the very edge of Alresford Creek is among the oldest buildings still standing in Alresford.

These cottages were known locally as the "Smugglers Cottages" because of a miniature creek that existed to the right of the building and led to an underground cellar known as the smugglers entrance. It was thought that this underground cellar extended under the whole of the building.

In 1930 a local builder carrying out painting and decorating work on the cottage discovered whilst stripping out old plasterwork a number of beautifully carved wooden panels depicting maritime scenes. These panels were sent to a leading auction house in London for valuation where they were found to be very valuable. To this day, nothing further is known about the whereabouts of these panels.

In the distance can be seen the All Saints Church at Brightlingsea.

PLUMPTONS FARM

Within this listed building, thought to be the oldest in Alresford, is an overhead beam bearing the date 1671 that can clearly be seen in the house, however, it is thought that an earlier building almost certainly existed on this site. Timber beams from abandoned boats have also been used in the construction of this building. Whilst the front part of the house, hidden behind a layer of red bricks is original 1671, the rear was enlarged in the 19th century by adding an outer skin of red bricks to avoid possible subsidence.

Plumptons, is ideally located close to the creek midway between the sand and gravel works and the nearby Thorrington Mill. The house and surrounding land was hit in 1953 by very severe flooding that affected many parts of the East Anglian coastline.

The water that is used for domestic purposes is still piped from wells that are located a short distance from the house, these wells were sunk in the 1940s and are examined every three years for water purity.

SEED HARVEST

In 1941 following a long line of previous owners, Thomas William Glover purchased the Thorrington Tide Mill. Son Thomas Frederick carried on the business of growing flowers and garden produce for seed, these when harvested were sold to major seed merchants.

In this photograph, Mrs Doris Glover is seen literally in a 'sea of flowers' with her son Thomas Alfred, (present owner); picking sweetpea pods. The seeds were then placed in a drier before packaging into small hessian bags, tied around their waists, these were then sent to various seed merchants. Other flowers and vegetables grown for seed harvesting were, wallflower, clarkia, pansy, runner beans and onions.

Notice the tide mill and house in the background. The business of growing flowers for their seeds finished approximately 1974.

WINDMILL

This copy of an old painting shows a windmill located at the end of Alresford Creek and can be dated back to 1675.
In 1869 this mill was so badly hit by a severe gale that it was reported in the "Essex Weekly News" of 24th December 1869.

The gale caused great havoc in this neighbourhood, many sheds being blown down and stacks unroofed.

Towards midnight the wind increased to hurricane force, efforts by men to prevent disaster by roping back the mill sails and shutters failed. So violent was the storm that Mr. Chopping 'owner of the mill' and his son and two other men ran great risk of losing their lives by holding on to the last, when the wind shaft snapped carrying with it four of the finest and most complete double-patents in Essex, the yard was strewn with huge timbers, the shutters flying in the air. It is wonderful, said Mr. Chopping, that not one of the four received any injury as three minutes earlier, they were holding a rope on the very spot where this great mass of shivered timbers and iron work fell.

As can be seen from the information I have given, Thorrington Tide-Mill and the associated Windmill were very important to this area, it is pleasing to know that the present building is now maintained by the Essex County Council and watched over by Mr. Tom Glover.

MILL HOUSE AND WINDMILL

THORRINGTON TIDE MILL

Barges seen here loading or unloading have almost certainly made a hazardous journey from the city with their cargoes of manure or lime for local farmers. In return, straw and hay would be sent back on barges' known as 'Stackies' to be used for feeding the heavy volume of horse traffic in London.

This mill has had no less than sixteen owners including one lady owner. Although the mill can be dated back to 1675 through previous owners, a mention by the great Essex historian 'Morant' states that a half-share in a watermill in the Alresford parish was left to a Mary Barwick in 1558. Could this be the mill shown on old maps of Alresford?

The nearby Brook indicates the boundary between Alresford and Thorrington.

DERELICT TIDE MILL

When Mr Thomas William Glover bought this mill in 1941 it was in a very dilapidated condition as can be seen in this picture. He set about restoring the building to its original condition putting in strengthening beams. The mill was used for drying and storing seeds from flowers grown on the estate. (See page 11)

    Notice the dilapidated condition of the mill. Brightlingsea All Saints Church is seen in the distance. The mill has been in the Glover family since 1941 and has now been taken over by the Essex County Council.

SOUTH LODGE, ALRESFORD

SOUTH LODGE

There were three lodges located in various parts of Alresford but little is known of any of them. It's possible they were built as homes for the employees of Alresford Hall. These small buildings are all different in style but South lodge was easily recognised by its thatched roof and two very prominent monkey-puzzle trees in the front garden.

The house was without a water supply or well, the occupants had to cart their water in milk churns from the nearby Plumpton's farm. In 1970 a deep sunk well was built on this site.

Sadly, the building was demolished in 1972.

Who is the gentleman just visible behind the front door? Do you recognise him?

LODGE FARM.

Following the end of the First World War 1914-18, many farm estates in the midlands and north of England were being broken up with many northern farmers migrating to the south of the country. Lodge Farm was purchased in 1919 by John Pilkington, he, with two brothers and sisters migrated with their parents from Lancashire to Alresford.

This farm could best be described as a general agricultural farm specializing in dairy farming as well as growing vegetables such as potatoes, cabbages etc. Barges from London and Colchester often anchored at the bottom of this farm to replenish their stocks of fresh water from springs located in the grounds of the farm.

The Military authorities commandeered Lodge Farm during the Second World War 1939/45 to site a searchlight battery. Italian prisoners of war were also hired to carry out essential farm labour at this farm.

Compare this postcard taken many years ago to the picture overleaf showing Lodge farm with its fine garden and beautiful surroundings overlooking the River Colne, very few changes appear to have been made to the outside of this building except that a tall chimney, small outbuildings, and two small windows in the front roof area have been removed.

LODGE FARM

RURAL SCENE

This delightful picture of a quiet tree lined lane in Alresford was probably designed as a postcard presumably for visitors to the village as a memento of their visit. However, local residents had traditions that had been handed down for generations, they were very proud of their village heritage and would almost certainly have purchased one of these cards.

What was life like when this photograph was taken? This narrow lane was used mainly for driving herds of cattle to and from their grazing meadows.

Whilst the horse and cart was the main mode of transport, the occasional motor-car was just appearing on our roads.

Notice the little girl and boy resting on the right of the road, who are they?

FORD LANE

GARDEN PRODUCE

Photograph shows a number of horse drawn carts and lorries at the rear of Alresford station presumably waiting to start their long and arduous journey to the London markets.

William Pilkington owned several lorries, Thorneycrofts, Scammels and Vulcans, all with solid tyres. They went to the London markets, Covent-Garden, Spitalfields and the Borough Market in all weathers and on at least one trip to London, when the snow and ice were very bad, they had occasion to lay sacks on the road to help them climb the hills.

Their meals en-route usually consisted of egg, beans and chips taken at a roadside cafe.

Loading of lorries was often carried out with assistance from Italian Prisoners of War. Some of these were very clever craftsmen and would often make baskets and rocking-horses for local children in exchange for a few cigarettes.

Leaving Alresford very early in the morning, these vehicles would arrive in London at about mid-day to unload their cargo of sugar-beet, cabbage, savoy, cauliflower, leeks, tomatoes, onions and lettuce. When unloaded, they made their way to the London docks to pick up animal foods and other items, finally arriving back in Alresford around 6.00 am the following morning.

This routine took place two to three times per week leaving little time for leisure activities, if indeed there were any.

Pictured left to right are: The Station Master, J.J.Pilkington, R.J.Pilkington, David Parker, Mr Everett, Bill Taylor, David Ashton, Charlie Simpson; Percy South, William Pilkington.

On the extreme left of picture can be seen the Pilkington's family dog.

GARDEN PRODUCE

LODGE HOUSE

This delightful and quaint little flint cottage, sometimes known as 'West Lodge', sits at the entrance to a narrow tree lined lane leading to the Alresford Hall estate. Beyond Alresford Hall, the lane continues to the nearby Quarter's house, home of Sir William and Lady Boulton.

Today, the lodge is a private house, it was originally built by the Hawkins family in a similar style to that of the small flint built school (see page 44) in Ford Lane and was probably the home of a gamekeeper in the employ of the Lord of the manor.

ALRESFORD HALL

Domesday Book, compiled in 1086, mentions two manorial estates in Alresford with different owners, later on these combined under the titles of the Manor of Alresford and Cockayne. In more recent times, Alresford Hall was regarded as the most important building in Alresford. Many lords of the manor have passed through these doors, none more so than Squire Matthew Martin, sea captain and director of the East India Company, who, as a result of his great achievement in the Indian Ocean, was awarded a very large sum of money.

His portrait is shown on page 25 this book.

The actual date when Alresford Hall was built remains unknown, however, prior to its arrival in Alresford, it was generally thought that a manor called 'Old Hall' existed not far from this site.

MATTHEW MARTIN

This special portrait depicts one of the most colourful characters in Alresford's history, Matthew Martin of Alresford Hall.

Early in the 18th century he was a ship's captain employed by the East India Company. While in command of the 32-gun armed merchantman, the "Marlborough", he was attacked by three French warships in the Indian Ocean. He fought them off bringing his vessel with its valuable cargo safely into Madras. For his gallantry in this battle, he was awarded a bonus of £1,000, presented with a gold medal set with 24 diamonds, and made a director of the Company. There was also talk of a knighthood, although he presented Queen Anne with a lion cub, he did not get a title. However, he made very good use of his bonus money and opportunities for profitable speculation were open to a director of the East India Company, for by 1720 he was rich enough to purchase Alresford Hall and set himself up as a country gentleman.

In the General Election of 1722, when Walpole came to power, Martin was elected as Whig M.P. for Colchester, defeating Isaac Rebow, who had held the seat for 33 years. Honours were showered upon him - a coat of arms incorporating the famous gold medal - Justice of the Peace - Deputy Lieutenant of Essex - High Steward of Colchester - and Mayor of Colchester in 1726. His career illustrates the way in which the ruling classes of those days opened their ranks to men of wealth.

In 1730, Matthew Martin performed a great service to local history by commissioning a map and survey of the parish of Alresford, this gave detailed information on every field and farm, their owners and occupiers. He let out all the land and the woods to tenants, but kept for his own use only "the fishponds and islands, walks, etc." near the Quarters House. In these peaceful surroundings, so far removed from the stress of maritime and financial victories, he died in 1749.

Notice the picture of a ship behind Matthew Martin. Is this the 'Marlborough'?

A stone slab marking his tomb can still be seen on the floor of the ruined St. Peter's Church.

THE QUARTERS HOUSE

This tranquil picture of the Quarters house that formed part of the Alresford Hall estate was mentioned in 'Morants History of Essex' in 1476 when it was originally thought to have been a mill cottage. The Mill referred to by Morant ceased to operate long ago and the only remaining trace is the lake and possibly the outflow ditches. It is thought it might have discontinued as a mill when the Thorrington Tide Mill came into being in the 17th century.

In 1772, Isaac Martin Rebow, owner of the Alresford Hall estate had the cottage transformed by the architect, Richard Wood into its present form, the main feature being the Chinese pagoda (fishing lodge) originally built out over the lake. The building still contained very little living space and when Sir Edward Boulton came to live here in 1952, he had a new section built on at the front which was so skilfully done that it is virtually impossible, from the outside, to distinguish the new from the old.

The question is sometimes asked, 'What is the origin of the name The Quarters?'

There was a story that troops were quartered here during the Siege of Colchester in 1648. A more likely explanation is that it resulted from the decision by the owners of the Alresford Hall to house employees e.g., grooms, woodmen and keepers in this house.

Present owners of the Quarters house, much respected by residents of Alresford, are Sir William and Lady Boulton.

THE QUARTERS HOUSE

THE "MISSING" CONSTABLE PAINTING

This picture of 'The Quarters House' painted in 1816 by landscape artist John Constable was kindly supplied by the 'National Gallery of Victoria' Australia.

John Constable wrote on August 21st, 1816 to Maria Bicknell (his fiancée and I quote from a copy of the original letter):

"My Dearest love, I returned from my very pleasant visit at General Rebow's on Monday . . . the General and Mrs Rebow are determined to be of some service to me . . . I am to paint two small landscapes for the General' one in the park (Wivenhoe) a house and a beautiful wood and piece of water; and another a wood with a little fishing house where the young lady (who is the heroine of all these scenes) goes occasionally to angle."

In 1816, landscape artist John Constable was commissioned by General F. Slater-Rebow of Wivenhoe Park, (now the Wivenhoe Conference Centre) who also owned the Alresford Hall estate, to do two small paintings, one of the Park (now in Washington, U.S.A.) the other of 'the Chinese style fishing lodge known as the Quarters' in nearby Alresford.

The latter was subsequently bought by a Glasgow schoolmaster, Benjamin Brookman, he emigrated to Australia around the middle of the 19th century. Benjamin Brookman left the painting to his son who in turn brought it back to England in 1890. The son had two daughters who lived together in London, along with the painting. In 1941, one sister was killed in an air-raid, the surviving sister, Mrs. Kirkpatrick, fearing further disaster took it to the Agent-General's office for Victoria (Australia) in London for safe keeping.

Mrs. Kirkpatrick died in 1958. In the same year Mr. Kirkpatrick, now back in Australia, read an article that appeared in the 'Times Newspaper' of the 18th September 1958 about the discovery of the painting and ownership enquiries, he remembered that he had seen this picture hanging in the family home at Mersham in Surrey, he contacted the Agent-General's Office in London, to say that this painting belonged to Mrs. Kirkpatrick who had originally wanted it to go back to Adelaide but had changed her mind in favour of the Art Gallery in Melbourne.

Mrs. Kirkpatrick's wish was granted and the painting was hung in the National Art Gallery in Melbourne where it remains to this day.

The painting returned to England briefly in 1976 for an exhibition at the Tate Gallery of John Constable's pictures.

The young lady referred to by Constable in his letter to Maria Bicknell,' who goes occasionally to angle' at the little fishing house was in fact Colonel Isaac Martin Rebow's granddaughter, it is clear that it was to the Alresford Hall Estate that she went.

THE "MISSING" CONSTABLE PAINTING

WIVENHOE PARK PAINTING

Landscape artist, John Constable, was in 1816, commissioned by General F. Slater-Rebow, to paint this picture of Wivenhoe Park, along with the Chinese Fishing Lodge at Alresford.

War Memorial, Alresford.

81635.

WAR MEMORIAL
ST. PETER'S CHURCH
ALRESFORD

To the gallant men of Alresford who sacrificed their lives in the 1st World War, the following message is inscribed:

TO THE GLORY OF GOD, AND IN HONOURED MEMORY OF THE ALRESFORD MEN WHO FELL IN THE GREAT WAR,
1914-1918.
ROWLAND PRICHARD, LIEUTENANT, SUFFOLK REGT.
GILES PRICHARD, LIEUTENANT, EAST YORKSHIRE REGT.
JOHN C. GRIMWOOD, LIEUTENANT.
PERCY MITCHELL, ESSEX REGT,
CHARLES RICE, ESSEX REGT,
LESLIE BUTTON, FREDERICK RICE,
WILLIAM GARRAD, R.N. PERCY MCKINLEY,
HERBERT ARNOLD, SUSSEX REGT,
JOHN FRANKLIN,
ROGER BACON, QUEEN'S WESTMINSTER RIFLES.
1939-1945 WAR.
H. D. COX, K. D. HART,
H.W.ELLIS, H. R. PRYKE, R. C. WERNHAM.

ST. PETER'S CHURCH

This old and rare photograph shows St. Peter's Church, standing on a hill overlooking the River Colne as it flows towards the estuary from its upper reaches and down to the Hythe port at Colchester. The church, only a short distance from the village centre is located in a quiet lane flanked by trees on either side, it forms an attractive feature in the surrounding countryside.

The church was built about 1320 by Anfrey de Staunton, who in 1312 obtained the manor of Alresford and the rites of the church.

Parishioners attending a Sunday morning service at a time when this picture was taken would see more top hats than could be seen in a twelve months period today. Ladies took advantage of this Sunday church service to show off their new hats, crinoline dresses and bustles, which at that time were just coming into fashion. Sadly, only a skeleton of this building is now left standing.

Who are the people at the fence and what are they so interested in? Any suggestions?

ST. PETER'S CHURCH

CHURCH WEDDING

A wedding is always a happy occasion. The couple getting married are Celia Fowler and Peter Sainty seen here in 1958 with the Reverend J. R. McCallum, taking their wedding vows

This beautiful picture of St. Peter's interior is greatly enhanced by the marriage ceremony that is taking place within the church. Following the service, a reception was held in the village hall, the music was usually supplied by means of a record player. How things have changed! Mr. Sydney Ennew, the local baker provided the catering for the wedding guests. Crowds of excited onlookers gathered at the gate to watch the newly weds re-appeared after the ceremony.

It's interesting to see the hatchments that adorned walls on either side of the church. Although this picture is shown in black and white, the lovely church windows can still be admired and appreciated.

CHURCH FIRE

This sad photograph taken one morning in October 1971 following the dreadful fire, clearly shows the total devastation to St. Peter's Church. The fire was discovered at 1.30 a.m. and fire engines from Colchester, Clacton, Brightlingsea, Weeley and Wivenhoe arrived to fight the blaze. The following day, the Church Harvest Festival had to be transferred to the Village Hall.

A building fund was quickly started in the village, but it was not known at the time whether to restore St. Peter's or build a new church. The latter was eventually decided and a new St. Andrews Church was built. The bell of St. Peter's was bought by Mistley Church in 1983. Part of the original font was incorporated into the new font at St. Andrews Church.

Alresford Old Church

ST. PETERS RUINS

Early in the morning of 2nd October 1971, this once beautiful Saxon Church of St. Peter's was totally destroyed by fire. Much speculation has arisen as to how the fire started, but no positive explanation has been given as to the actual cause of the fire.

   Although the picture above was taken some time after the fire, it does however, show clearly the extent of damage to the church.

   In earlier days St. Peter's church was well supported and would always be full to capacity, if you were late in arriving at the church, it would be difficult to find a seat except under the gallery.

   The ruins of St. Peter's Church will always remain a permanent memorial and reminder to the residents of Alresford.

ROBERT BRAY'S TOMB

One might think this picture of Robert Bray's tombstone dated 1724 seems a strange subject for a book about village life! It appears to be the oldest grave in Alresford churchyard, however, because this is a picture that raises some curiosity and interesting comments, I feel it deserves an inclusion in this book.

In 1678, an act known as the 'Burial in Woolen Act' was designed to protect the important English wool trade. This act in particular stated that no corpse of any person shall be buried in any shirt, shift, sheet or shroud or anything whatsoever made or mingled with flax, hemp, silk, hair, gold or silver, or anything other than what is made of sheep's wool only. A statement was required to be sworn within a few days of the burial that the deceased had indeed been buried in woollens only, and this to be recorded in the burial register. If it was proven that a woolen burial had not taken place, a penalty of £5.00 was imposed.

People who died in the plague were exempt from the wool rule, (a skull and crossbones on stone, denoted that a person was not buried in wool.) The woolen act was repealed in 1814.

What does this crossbones inscription mean? Is there a connection with the Woolen Act?

Alresford Rectory.

ALRESFORD RECTORY

Many rectors and their families have lived in this building. One such person was the colourful Rev. William Charles Bache who was very active in this parish. A very tall man, he used to ride horseback through the village on a cream coloured horse, his feet almost touching the ground. He kept many necessities for any eventuality caused by sickness, such as blankets, sheets, bed linen, also an invalid chair ready for any resident in need. He was always ready to offer and give assistance to any of his parishioners.

After the Rev. W.C. Bache, 1877 came the Rev. C. C. Prichard, 1907, (he built the Cabin); Rev. W. A. Ferguson, 1919; Rev. H. M. Vivet, 1922; Rev. G. S. Duncan, 1932; Rev. C. J. Edwards, 1933; Rev. S. S. Huskisson, 1943; Rev. J. R. McCallum, 1945-69; Rev. A. H. Smith, 1970-79.

STAINED GLASS WINDOW

This nostalgic group photograph was taken on the occasion of a special service that was held in St. Peter's Church following the end of the First World War to dedicate a beautiful stained glass window to the memory of two sons of the late Rev. Charles Colwyn Prichard, Rowland and Giles, they were killed in action during the 1914/18 War.

Pictured centre front row are: The Bishop of either Colchester or Chelmsford. To his left is the Rev. Anthony Hammond, vicar of Elmstead, he acted as Bishop's Chaplain at the ceremony.

Rev. Prichard is second left, back row. Rev. Prichard's wife is seated front row to the right of the Bishop.

PRICHARD FAMILY PORTRAIT

The Reverend Charles Colwyn Prichard, pictured here with his wife and family, in the rectory grounds at Alresford, was born at Burlish House, Stourport in 1846.

By 1851, the young Charles Prichard had travelled with his parents to New Zealand. Here, he became a pupil at the Christ Church College. In 1870, after leaving Oxford College, he was ordained a Curate at Rugby. Having travelled to many parishes throughout England, the Reverend Prichard finally became Rector of Alresford from 1907-1918.

Pictured left to right are: Monty, Margie, Frank, Rowland, and Giles. Front row are: The Reverend and Mrs. Prichard.

ALRESFORD MOTHER'S UNION

The 'Alresford Mothers Union' was founded in 1910.

This photograph taken between 1912/14 shows a group of proud ladies from the Mothers Union posing outside the 'Cabin' located in the rectory grounds

In the picture back row left to right are: Mrs. Barr, Mrs. Everett, Mrs. Easter, Mrs. Bush. Middle row: Mrs. Baker, Mrs. Humphrey, Mrs. Vessy, Miss. Spooner, Mrs. Taylor, Miss. Prichard (Rectors daughter), Mrs. South, Mrs. Pittock. Front row: Mrs. Bush (senior), Mrs. Wells, Mrs. Barton, (Church Warden's Wife), Mrs. Prichard, (Rectors Wife), Mrs. Grimwood (Church Wardens Wife), Mrs. Blizzard, and Mrs. Miller.

THE CABIN

The 'Cabin' as it was affectionately known was built by the Rev. Prichard at his own expense, for the benefit of the parishioners of Alresford, this gift was very much appreciated by the village. It became the centre for most of the social activities that took place in Alresford, many organisations still existing today started their life here.

Situated at the entrance to the old rectory, it was generally intended for use by the church, however, many other social events including regular whist drives took place in this building.

After the rector's death in 1918, Mrs. Prichard presented the cabin to the Rev. Edwards to be used for the general use of the public.

A new village hall has long since been provided, although the cabin does still exist, it is no longer used by residents of Alresford.

CHURCH FARM

Church Farm, pictured here was typical of most farms in the early 19th century. Alresford was a tiny rural village having a small population of farmers whose workers generally lived with their families in tied cottages.

When Queen Victoria came to the throne in 1837, Alresford was still mainly a farming community. Church farm was first in the village to install an irrigation system with pumps to its fields. In the early years, this farm was involved with dairy farming, it also specialised in potatoes, peas, runner beans, and cabbages, which carried on until the late 1950s. Mr. Ian Hodge, owner of Church Farm, was described by a lady who worked these fields, as a *'Gentleman Farmer'* frequently asking the ladies how they were getting on, and taking a general interest in their general welfare, he also made it clear that whilst he understood they occasionally took some produce home at the end of the day, he didn't mind so long as they were not feeding the entire road.

Residents taking their Sunday stroll in Ford Lane would often encounter a herd of cows heading in their direction coming from, or going to, their grazing meadows.

CHURCH SCHOOL, 1846.

Prior to the building of this Church of England School in Ford Lane, many other types of education existed in different parts of England and Wales. For example, there were 'Monitorial Schools', 'Factory Schools' and the 'Ragged & Industrial Schools' these were founded in 1844.

This attractive National School in Ford Lane was purpose built to accommodate 80 children of mixed sexes. The School was erected in 1846 by the generosity of William Warwick Hawkins and presented to this parish in 1896 by Mrs. Hawkins. The Head Governess (mistress) at this school in 1862 was Mrs. Charlotte Watsham followed in 1908 by Mrs. Knight. There was also Miss Amelia Chignall, she was employed at a salary of £50 per year and according to reports by the late Mr. Albert Carter, this lady did a very fine job, she was greatly respected by all members of the community, and lived to the great age of 92 years.

CHURCH SCHOOL, 1913.

This photograph was taken outside the small flint Church School in Ford Lane. The little girl seen on the extreme right of the picture front row is, Gladys Edith Welham, granddaughter of Samuel Welham, a fisherman who lived in Copyhold Cottage located at the edge of the river Colne. In 1866 the Tendring Hundred Railway Company built a new line that passed within only a few yards of their cottage. Gladys was born in 1905. This photograph must have been taken around 1913. Her grandfather Samuel Welham, died tragically at sea, near Plymouth, in 1897.

One year later, another member of the Welham family, a fisherman like his father, also named Samuel Welham, met a tragic death at the age of 42 whilst trying to recover one of the family fishing boats alongside the river Colne, it had been driven ashore in the high tide of 1897. Whilst clearing mud from beneath the boat in 1898, it keeled over on its side burying Samuel beneath.

SCHOOL GROUP, 1900.

This photograph taken about 1900 of a group of nearly sixty school children posing in Ford Lane must be one of the first school pictures taken in Alresford. Close scrutiny of this photograph show that hardly any of the children are smiling, they have been told to remain perfectly still whilst the cameraman took his picture. Bearing in mind that photography was very much in its infancy, this is another remarkable and nostalgic picture. The girls in their smocks and bonnets, the boys in their breeches all appear to look the same. Was this a recognised school uniform?

Who is the man at the gate? Could the person standing in the doorway be the Reverend Bache who, sixteen years earlier, had been present in the school on the morning of the Great Essex Earthquake in 1884?

SCHOOL GROUP, 1909.

Postcard taken almost 100 years ago shows pupils of the Church School, located in a quiet part of Ford Lane posing to have their group photograph taken for posterity.

The picture was taken so long ago that unfortunately it is not possible to name the children. Also note that the children are still not smiling for the photographer. This was no accident, the children were instructed to stand or sit still and not to smile, this action was considered unfashionable at that time, the art of photography having been in existence for approximately fifty years.

SCHOOL GROUP, 1921.

A group photograph taken around 1921 showing pupils posing in the grounds of Church School. Notice how much the styles of dress have changed from earlier school pictures shown in this book. Notice also the three little girls in the front row, they appear to be clasping a stick, each adorned with flowers.

Pictured back row, left to right are: Cis Girt, Ivy Clarke, Rebecca Parker, Florence Blundon, Clara Girt, and Florence South.

Front row left to right are: Young boy, Gladys Farthing, Elma Cox, Ruth Metson, and Charles Miles.

SCHOOL GROUP, 1935/8.

This picture taken sometime between 1935-38 shows pupils in the Church School grounds posing for the photographer. Unlike the earlier picture of 1909, the children with their teacher Miss Last are now allowed to smile a little for the photographer. Notice how in those few years, the styles of dress have changed, the lace and starched collars on some of the boys have gone as have smocks and ribbons on the girls.

Pictured extreme left is class teacher, Miss Last. Pictured back row second from right is Joan Emeney. Brother's Horace and Rowly Emeney are also in this picture.

SCHOOL GROUP, 1956.

A more recent picture taken around 1956 shows a class of pupils with their teacher Miss Last in the playground of Church school in Ford Lane.

VILLAGE HALL COMMITTEE

Following discussions concerning the future use of a small wooden building in Ford Lane known locally as 'The Cabin', Alresford residents decided to raise as much money as possible to build a new village hall. Dances and Fetes were held in the grounds of Alresford Hall, home of Mr. G. Cobbold. Ladies made door-to-door collections to raise more funds.

The whole building was, after two years' hard work eventually erected at a cost £700. Mr. G. F. Cobbold, was chairman of the village hall committee. Brigadier-General Kincaid-Smith said that the erection of a hall was a big step forward in the village, and all who had helped towards creating the building deserved the warmest congratulations.

Pictured Back row, left to right are: William Pilkington, Mr. Bills, Mac Watson, John Humphrey, and Albert Carter. Front row, left to right are: Phil Barr, George Baker, Guy Cobbold, Brigadier General, Kinkaid Smith, Mrs. Kinkaid Smith, this gentleman cannot be not identified.

SCHOOL CONCERT

This photograph of the annual Christmas Nativity Play was taken in 1956 at the old school house in Ford Lane. Unfortunately, several names are missing, however, some of the performers have been identified and are listed below.

Back row, left to right are: Eileen South, Susan Pentney, Jackie Fowler, Middle row, left to right are: not known. Front row, third from left are: Roger Carter, Pauline Mellish, and Valerie Nunn.

CHILDREN'S OUTING

This photograph taken in 1957 of a Methodist Church outing shows a group of happy children enjoying a warm summer day with their carer Mrs. Florrie Goodwin, they are seen here posing on the beach at the seaside resort of Walton on the Naze.

Pictured from left to right are most of the children: Christopher Goodwin, Geoffrey Goodwin, Jennifer Marshall, Christine Smith, Angela Smith, Rosemary Pannel, Gerald Cox, Susan Starline, Andrew Cox, Diane Marshall, and David Calver.

ALRESFORD OPTOMISTS

This photograph shows a sea of happy faces following a pantomime performance in the village hall of 'Robin Hood' by the Alresford 'Optomists'. This talented and successful charity fund raising group have been entertaining various organisations throughout the district for many years.

Pictured left to right are: Producer, Marion Caine; Accordion, Sharon Crick; Angela Crick, Jenny Hughes, Richard Davey, Lorna Burling, Derick Newbold, Margaret Clubb, Joan Clarke, Wendy Wilson, Chris Stiffel, Brian Wilson, Irene Dickinson, Mabel Sugget, Pianist, Vivian Knowles. Children: Rachel Turner, Francis Wilson, Cathy Burling, Sarah Newbold, Rebecca Sawers, Emma Neubronner, Clair Ward, Nichola Trangmar, and Alison Cable.

VILLAGE BABY SHOW

These proud mothers are seen posing in 1952-3 with their babies at the annual church fete held in the grounds of the old rectory. The Reverend J. R. McCallum was present at this event, as was Doctor Craig of Great Bentley who judged the competition. Doctor Wiltshire and Nurse Bennett can be seen centre row.

Thirty or so years ago, no fete or village event would seem the same without a baby show. How does one judge a baby or indeed pick a winner? Surely, every mother would consider her own child to be the best in the show.

Because I am unable to accurately name all of these mothers, I feel I must refrain from naming any of them. Do you recognise anyone in this picture?

CHURCH CHOIR.

The Church Choir that was formed many years ago are seen here performing at one of their annual concerts. They suffered a major setback following the dreadful fire of 1971 which completely gutted and devastated St. Peter's Church, however, the choir reformed again giving much pleasure to many people. The choir Mistress for most of this period was Mrs. Whistlecraft.

Annual concerts such as 'Oklahoma' were presented by this choir and were supported by large audiences. Local bands usually supplied the appropriate musicical support.

Pictured from left to right are: Penny Carter, Margaret Nunn, Marion Birch, Janet Farthing, Suzanne Pentney, Lucy Grimwood, Valerie Nunn, Shirley Cooper, Jackie Fowler, Christine Rowlands, Paula Fowler and Eileen Appleby.

OLD CODGERS

The late Charlie Farthing was in 1932 Captain and founder member of the Alresford Colne Rangers Football Club from which the 'Old Codgers' is so derived. They quickly developed and joined the Brightlingsea and District League in 1936-37. This photograph taken in the 1970s shows the 'Old Codgers' posing for the cameraman on Q.B. Printers playing field.

Alresford F.C. are a friendly village club with a strong sense of tradition as stated by club Chairman, Alan Green, he recently received a long-service award from Essex County F.A.

Pictured back row, left to right are: Bruce Ridgers, Brian Matthews, George Newley, Norman Sibbons, Jimmy Riley, Peter Sainty, Peter Carrington. Front row, left to right are: Brian Light, Mick Barker, John Kent, Roger Goodwin, Bernie Thompson, Ray Milburn.

ALRESFORD EAGLES

This more recent picture of the 'Alresford Eagles' as these boys were known shows a happy group of aspiring young boys posing for the cameraman on the village playing field behind the village hall.

Pictured back row, left to right are: Craig Finbow, Lee Hammond, Russell Dupre, Wayne Mathias. Centre row left to right are: Scott Ridgers, Kevin Richards, James Morton, Andy Burbridge, Kieron Johnston. Front row left to right are: Paul Simons, Steven O'Mara, Chris Chappelhow, Matt Page and Billy Roberts.

LADIES KEEP FIT GROUP

Keep Fit Ladies are seen here proudly posing in their costumes at the Alresford carnival.

Mrs. Ena Adams was a founder member of the 'Keep Fit Group' that was formed around 1967-68. Unfortunately, it is not possible in this book to show them in their bright scarlet costumes.

Pictured back row, left to right are: Janet Chapman, partially hidden is Sheila Kirton; Eileen Rainbird, Ann Milburn, Celia Sainty, Margaret Moss, Mary Sibbons, Joan Unwin, Rachael Martin, Beryl Tickner, and Midge Thompson.

Front row, left to right are: Edna Butcher, Sandra Gray, Cicely Birch, Pat Burmby, and Lesley Adams.

ALRESFORD JOGGERS.

Alresford Joggers were originally started mid 1970s by Mr. Bill Pratt who began his athletic career in the early 1930s. At 69 years of age Bill was the oldest runner to compete in the Harwich and Colchester Marathons. After being wounded during the Second World War, Bill thought his running career was finally finished, however, he managed to make a remarkable comeback. Serving his sport for nearly fifty years Bill was well qualified to lead the Alresford joggers; three runners from this club actually ran the London Marathon.

Pictured back row, left to right are: Tony Harrison, Nigel Harridge, Bill Pratt, Sam Longstreet, Kevin Lindguard, Bill McArthur. Centre row, left to right are: Sandra Barnard, Jan Betts, Marilyn Harridge, Vina Corton, Gillian Light, Vida Riley, Lynne Thorne. Front row, left to right are: Tracy Smith, Kathy McArthur, Beryl Ridgers, Tom Longstreet.

HEATHER COTTAGE

Heather Cottage located in Church Road, originally a dairy farm, is believed to date from the 17th century. Old maps show this building as Heath Farm located in the parish of Alresford. Described as a 'Three Bay Cottage' meant that the house was equipped with three rooms each measuring 13 square feet.

Whilst the gardens of Heather Cottage have been used over the years for various social events such as fetes etc, the barn was also used at the turn of the century as a temporary school room whilst alterations were being carried out on the nearby church school.

The past 150 years have seen extensive alterations to this building many of which were carried out by local builder Mr. George Baker.

1ST. ALRESFORD GUIDE COMPANY

The 1st Alresford Girl Guide Company that was formed in the 1950s held their early meetings in a barn at Heather Cottage, Church Road. Pictured in the garden of Heather cottage can be seen the first guide enrolment ceremony being carried out in Alresford.

The young guide being enrolled by the District Commissioner is Eunice Fowler. Behind Eunice is Mabel Sallows, Lieutenant. Margaret Fitch, Founder and Captain, is seen behind the District Commissioner. These ladies with Paula Fowler have played a leading role in successfully running this guide company for many years. Extreme left can be seen Mr. and Mrs. Daly, local café owners who donated flags to both guide and scout companies.

1ST ALRESFORD GUIDE COMPANY

This photograph taken early in the 1950s show a happy gathering of Alresford girl guides displaying a fine selection of preserves and garden produce in the grounds of the old rectory in Ford Lane. Pictured left to right are: Christine Rowlands, Margaret Pennell, Ann Hubbard, Margaret Hubbard, Mrs. Margaret Fitch; Eunice Fowler, Jenny Burbage, Anne Jennings, and Janice Fowler.

ALRESFORD PRIMARY SCHOOL

Postcard shows a modern Alresford primary school surrounded by trees. Built in 1963, it replaced the small flint built school further down Ford Lane.

Mrs. Warren, who had previously been mistress at the old school, carried on as headmistress at the new school for the next five years. She finally retired having faithfully served the parish of Alresford for sixteen years.

Other headmaster's at this school have been Mr. James who retired in 1987. Mr. Kemp, and Mr. R. Newman. Mr. R. Newman is the current headmaster.

Alresford Church

ST. ANDREWS CHURCH

St. Andrew's Church was dedicated in 1976 as a direct result of the terrible fire of 1971 that totally devastated and destroyed the once beautiful early Norman or Saxon Church of St. Peter's. Although it is not possible to compare or replace St. Peter's Church, the new church is however, a pleasant multi-purpose, much used and attractive building sited nearer the main part of the village and backing on to lush open meadows surrounded by trees.

Many local events particularly suited to St. Andrew's Church that have taken place are: floral displays, photographic and art and craft exhibitions.

The Minister for the millennium is the Reverend Christopher Harvey.

ALRESFORD

FORD LANE COTTAGES

Taken around 1920 this postcard shows boarded cottages looking towards Meads corner. Located in Ford lane just below the village hall, this cottage was divided into three separate homes. Notice the little boy standing at the garden gate. He is thought to be the late Charlie Farthing, founder member of the Alresford Colne Rangers football team and once a gardener at the Grange for Wilson Marriage.

Although these boarded cottages were demolished many years ago to make way for new developments, they are still remembered with affection by many residents.

Jones' — 1906

WIVENHOE ROAD, 'MEADS CORNER'

When this picture was taken in 1906 the main road through Alresford had not yet been built, there was to be a period of some thirty years before this came into being. The only mode of transport at this time was either the horse or bicycle, assuming you were able to afford one.

In towns and cities throughout the country the popular mode of travel was by horse and cart or the horse drawn trams, motor-cars were just starting to appear on our roads. However, this small group of people standing outside Mead's shop had probably never been outside their village and had little idea of the changes that were taking place around them. In rural villages such as Alresford, horses were used mainly for agricultural purposes rather than for transportation.

Notice the dress styles and particularly the real fox fur around the lady's shoulders, today, this would perhaps, not be considered correct. Who are the people in the picture?

CHARABANC OUTING

This postcard taken much later shows a charabanc at the junction of Wivenhoe Road, Ford Lane and Coach Road. The corner was for many years affectionately known as 'Meads' Corner' named after its owners. Today, it is known as 'Jones' Corner.

The charabanc seen here with its solid tyres appears to be carrying among its passengers several members of the Alresford Silver Band, are they on their way to entertain at a village fete?

Although this shop is now closed, there has been a business on this site for 150 years. For much of this time it was the village post office.

NORTH LODGE.

This photograph displays an attractive timber boarded building known locally as North Lodge, affectionately known as the 'Gingerbread Cottage'. Little is known of this cottage except that two other lodge cottages existed, it is thought that both this lodge and South Lodge shown on page 16 of this book formed part of the Alresford Hall estate.

Was the lodge located at the entrance of the lane leading to Alresford manor, pictured page 22 known as the West Lodge?

CHILDREN IN WIVENHOE ROAD

Baytree Cottage, partially hidden behind a tree, and 'Crestlands House' seen in the foreground, form a splendid backdrop for this delightful picture taken at the turn of the century. This building was erected in 1788 by local blacksmith Samuel Clarke. A plaque bearing his initials and date is set into the front wall of this house.

For 130 years, the Grimwood family have continued to run a blacksmith's business on this site.

Several generations of Grimwoods have been blacksmiths. This cottage, typical of buildings erected at that time has been extensively renovated over the years and it originally had two staircases, a large bread-oven, and possibly a forge.

There is so much to see in this interesting picture, notice that the children have been specially positioned across the road for the photographer, the smocks that the young ladies are wearing and breeches that the boys on the right are wearing give some indication of the period when this picture was taken.

CHILDREN IN WIVENHOE ROAD

WIVENHOE ROAD FORGE

In days when horses were the main source of power in farming and transport, every village had its own blacksmith. The earliest record of a forge in Alresford is 1730 when permission was granted to Samuel Clarke to erect a forge on part of Alresford Heath.

In 1855, James Grimwood with his son William took over the forge in Wivenhoe Road, it remained in the family until it was taken over by the late Walter Grimwood, he was Alresford's last blacksmith as well as 'being' churchwarden and village constable. Remains of the smithy's forge and bellows could still be seen as late as the 1950s.

The late Walter Grimwood was the last member of his family to live in this cottage.

FANMANS FARM.

Events such as Coronation festivities and various sports were held in the meadows of this farm. 'May Day' would ensure that young girls of the village would dress up in their garlands and parade through the village singing their songs.

Fanmans Farm was home to two authors; Pat Fluker better known as Emily Nash, her book entitled "Strawberries and Wine" told the story of a relationship between a modern girl named Cassie and Johnny a Second World War pilot.

Mary Norton was responsible for the book 'Bedknobs and Broomsticks', later turned into a film. She also wrote 'The Borrowers'.

Mr. Thomas Dandy from London planted the first apple orchard at Fanmans farm in 1947, up until that time these fields had been grazing meadows.

BROOK FARM

Brook Farm, located in St. Osyth Road was another dairy farm, having a herd of 125 cows. Income was supplemented by growing potatoes, and general garden produce. Apples from a nearby orchard were transported and sold to the Stratford market. Cows were machine milked at Brook farm twice daily. The movement of cattle between farm and grazing meadow was the responsibility of two farm workers who had to take great care when crossing main roads, opening and closing gates that separated the meadows. This was the case when cattle were driven from Brook farm to Marsh Farm located at the other end of the village. This farm was hired specifically to rear young livestock.

In the 1970s, a decline in the dairy farming industry commenced. Today, no cattle are kept in the parish of Alresford.

HIGH ELMS FARM

Known today as Tenpenny farm, 'High Elms' was once the home of Mr. Ralph Pilkington who came to Alresford from Lancashire with his family in the early 1930s. Like his brother who purchased Lodge farm, he too was a garden produce farmer growing many varieties of vegetables, these were conveyed twice a week to the London markets by his brother William who conveniently owned the garage just around the corner on the main road.

   The vehicles, used to convey this produce were equipped with solid tyres. Many roads in the 1930s were unmade, so the long journey to and from London must have been very uncomfortable indeed.

The Corner Café
Elmstead Heath, Colchester

ALRESFORD CAFÉ

This attractive café was originally owned and managed by Mr. and Mrs. Wright. In 1938, they sold the business on to Frank and Agnus Daly. In 1939, the 2nd World War commenced bringing with it many restrictions and changes. The main road to the east coast closed to traffic which affected trade considerably, however, it did bring many soldiers into Alresford and Mr. and Mrs. Daly found themselves supplying late night suppers, and making many cups of tea costing 2d per cup, coffee 3d, a boiled egg between 4d and 5d.

The sketch above, one of many, illustrates the attractive café located on the main Colchester to Clacton road, note how patriotic the owners were, the Union flag in the forecourt is surely testimony to this.

In 1958-59 Mr. Harold Norrington called here and learnt that the café was up for sale, following discussions with the owners, he decided that he would like to buy the business. Although these premises are now run as a general store, it is still affectionately known as 'Norringtons'

MR. JIM BIRD

Mr. Jim Bird, a local village character, is pictured here with his granddaughter, Joan Wingrave and two little girls. They are Anthea and Joy Harvey from Heath Farm. These two children were here because of a small donkey that Mr. Bird kept in his meadow. Anthea and Joy would often cross the main Colchester Road to see and feed this lovable animal.

Prior to the late 1950s, Jim's official address would have been Elmstead Heath, however, the boundaries have since changed and this part is now known as Alresford.

Jim would often be seen standing at his garden gate alongside the main road watching the traffic passing his house, he was always pleased when anyone stopped to hold a conversation.

ALRESFORD BAKERY

In this early 1930s picture of the Alresford bakery originally known as 'Prospect House', Mr. George Wells, owner of the bakery for many years is seen standing in the gateway.

By 1934, Mr. Sydney Ennew who had previously worked for Mr. Wells prior to joining the Merchant Navy, took over and ran this bakery. Starting with only one oven, Mr. Ennew quickly developed and built up a business employing many local residents. By the late 1940s, he had three shops, Wivenhoe, Brightlingsea and Alresford, where everything was baked. His van also delivered bread and cakes to many outlying districts around Alresford.

Branching out into the catering side, his special catering staff attended many functions. Saturdays especially would be extremely busy with perhaps as many as three weddings during the day and two dinners in the evening. All of the meals and cakes were cooked in their own ovens.

Fifty years on, people coming to buy flowers from Michael Ennew often ask the question: 'Was your father Syd Ennew? He did my wedding reception and cake!'

ALRESFORD BAKERY

SHOPPING PRECINCT.

Early in the 1960s, houses started to replace orchards and Alresford was fast being transformed from a quiet rural and agricultural village into a busy commuter region.

The railway line and station in the centre of the village was able to provide a fast link between Alresford and London which made this project a very popular choice with families who wanted to move away from the cities and towns.

Before and up to the 1960s Alresford had relied mainly on its garden produce, dairy and fruit growing abilities whilst at the same time providing much needed employment to residents of the village. This postcard indicates the necessity for a small shopping area to provide a service to these additional families who had arrived from various parts of the country including London.

Many varieties of fruits have been, and are still grown at Cockaynes and Fanmans. It is not then surprising that many roads in the village have been named after various types of apple, and in one particular instance, Orchard Road.

Hunters store seen in the foreground was one of the first shops to be built on the estate, notice the yet unmade Station Road.

STATION ROAD, ALRESFORD.

SHOPPING PRECINCT.

RAIL CROSSING KEEPER

This millennium photograph shows Pauline Hunt, a familiar and popular figure in the village of Alresford opening the railway crossing gates to allow trains through the village as they wend their way to Colchester, or the seaside resorts of Clacton on Sea, Frinton-on-Sea, or Walton on the Naze.

Although railway traffic only came to Alresford in 1866, it was some seventy years before a pedestrian bridge, seen behind Pauline was erected. There was great excitement one Sunday in 1937 when many local residents turned out for this great occasion to see a giant crane lift the bridge into its present position.

ALRESFORD STATION

Alresford Station, part of the Wivenhoe Weeley branch line, was officially opened in January 1866 by the Tendring Hundred Railway Company.

This photograph taken a few years later, shows a train fast approaching the station with a cloud of smoke emanating from its funnel.

Notice the absence of passengers on the platform. Is this a train just passing through?

On the left can be seen the existing main station building with its waiting room whilst on the opposite side can be seen a second waiting room, now demolished. A signal box can be seen at the far end of the platform.

RAILWAY STATION STAFF

This picture taken in the late 19th century shows members of the station staff posing for the photographer in front of their newly built station house.

The station staff can be seen proudly showing off their new uniforms outside the newly constructed building. Are they possibly waiting to be inspected?

The coming of the railway system to Alresford must have made a considerable difference to residents who had earlier been unable to venture far beyond Alresford. Prior to this very important event, travel to and from the village was somewhat restricted.

PARK FARM ORCHARD

This rural picture taken in 1947-8 shows Mr. J. E. Sidgwick, the farmer, and members of his fruit picking force, taking a well-earned break from their work.

Residents of Alresford have, for many years relied on the fruit picking industry as a main source of employment in the village. Pictured back row, left to right are: Arthur Watling, Reg Wingrave, Ken Blake, Rowland Emeney, Walter Farthing, Walter Blake, and Martin Ashbolt.

Seated front row, left to right are: Olly Farthing, Mrs. Birch, Babs Lawrence, Joan Blunden, Mr. J. E. Sidgwick, Phylis Gunn, Mrs. Mills, Joan Wingrave, and Linda Haynes.

COCKAYNES FARM

The present Cockaynes Farm was built in 1871. Over this long period, there has been much rebuilding and many changes of ownership, however, this farm has always been lived in by someone with a direct interest in the farming of its surrounding land.

Whilst apples have for many years been the main industry at Cockaynes, it must not be forgotten that potatoes have also been very important to the people of Alresford, as many as thirty or more ladies were employed here and will remember with affection the fun and teamwork shared whilst working these fields.

Apple orchards at Cockaynes and Fanmans have for many years proved very successful. Sadly, this industry at the moment appears to be in a decline.

Apples have been grown here at Cockayes since 1937. Mr. Robin Grinsted continued the business in 1972. Cockaynes and Fanmans orchards are now managed by David Grinsted.

COCKAYNES FARM

POINTER INN

Originally built as two cottages, this building has been a central landmark of Alresford for many years and can be dated back to 1770 or even much earlier. There is a reference to a 'disorderly' Ale House at Alresford in the quarter session records of 1618, it is not however, certain whether this refers to the 'Pointer'.

A tithe map of 1770 shows the 'Pointer', a 'Coaching Inn' as being an 'Ale House' called the Chequers', it may have been one long before that.

There have been several suggestions as to the origin of the name 'Chequers.' An article appearing in a prominent field magazine in 1976 stated that there was a clear connection between public houses named Chequers and the Chequer bush, or wild service tree, (Pyrus torminalis) The berries of this plant, it seems, were used to flavour beer prior to the introduction of hops into this country about the middle of the sixteenth century.

The old moneychangers used boards divided up into squares like modern chess boards, the sign of the 'CHEQUERS' may have originated, partly in these 'exchequers,' as they were then called, being hung up outside their place of business.

Another explanation offered was that at the turn of the century, drinkers would ask for a mixed beer consisting of half brown and half pale beer hence the word chequer.

"THE POINTER", ALRESFORD.

THE POINTER INN

CORONATION CEREMONY

The Pointer Inn is the setting for this tree planting ceremony. Local residents have turned out in numbers to participate with the Reverend J. R. McCallum in dedicating this tree on the occasion of the Coronation of H.M. Queen Elizabeth II in 1953.

The Coronation was an event that everyone wanted to celebrate. Television in 1953 was in its early life and few people were lucky enough to possess this wonderful piece of technology. However, an electrical engineer from nearby Wivenhoe kindly set up a television appliance in the village hall so that residents were able to gather round and share this great occasion together.

Other events that took place in the village included a variety show performed by the Alresford Scout and Guide companies.

Wivenhoe Road

WIVENHOE ROAD

This postcard shows the route that vehicles going to Clacton or Walton would have taken prior to the construction in 1937 of a road bridge crossing the main railway line.

During the summer months, vehicles on their return journey from Clacton to Colchester would be seen bumper to bumper along this section of road. 'Stop-Me-and-Buy-One' ice cream merchants took advantage of this situation and frequently peddled the contents of their tricycles to the drivers who were sitting in their cars patiently waiting for the level crossing gates to open.

Notice the large chestnut tree on the right. This was planted to commemorate the Diamond Jubilee of H.M. Queen Victoria in 1887.

WIVENHOE ROAD. ALRESFORD.

WIVENHOE ROAD, BOTTLE & GLASS

This postcard shows a quiet section of road leading from Alresford to Wivenhoe. On the left-hand side of the road partially hidden by trees can be seen a house, thought to have been an old beer house, named the 'Bottle & Glass'. Little is known of this building but this theory is borne out by the fact that, engraved in the plaster above the front of this building is the date 1737. Below this engraving is a picture illustrating a 'Bottle & Glass'.

A public house named the 'Ship at Launch' is listed in a directory of 1837.

An Ordnance Survey map of 1923 shows a building named the 'Ship House' located at exactly this location. Could this have been an Inn or Ale House?

ALRESFORD SILVER BAND

A local newspaper in 1958 described the Alresford Silver Band as something of a phenomenon. While other bands, from bigger centres, faded away through lack of support and waning interest, Alresford Silver Band, in their smart red, blue and gold uniforms and with their silver instruments gleaming in the sunshine, marched on merrily.

Beginning in the very early part of the twentieth century, the band began as an orchestra. It was re-formed, as Alresford United Brass Band, in 1910. Mr. Alfred Cansdale became secretary in 1919, when the fortunes of the band were at low ebb. He set about building up the financial soundness of the band and by 1921 had met with such success that the band became owners of a set of silver band instruments, the name was then changed to the 'Alresford Silver Band'. In the early days, Mr. Frank Watcham, who was a signalman at Alresford Station, was bandmaster and one of the founder members.

Since then, members of the band have played at fetes, garden parties, gymkhanas and carnivals in practically every parish in North Essex.

ALRESFORD SILVER BAND

The Silver Band, pictured in the grounds of Alresford Grange in their red, blue and gold uniforms are displaying their gleaming silver instruments. Apart from money raised from carrying out professional engagements, each member paid sixpence per week towards the cost of hiring a hall for weekly rehearsals and for uniforms and instruments. The original uniforms were blue and silver and were replaced by the more colourful ones seen in this picture. Funding was mainly by performances at garden fetes, carnivals, and British Legion services.

Twenty-three bandsmen are pictured here. Sixteen have been identified: John Humphrey, Bert Humphrey, Earnest Wayland, George Jennings, Walter Marshall, Percy Cardy, Alf Jennings, Jim Bush, Rupert Watcham, Percy South, Frank Watcham, Bandmaster; Freddie Goldacre, Joe South, Earnest Knott, Alf Cansdale, and Earnest Jennings. Seated, third right is Mr. Wilson Marriage.

WILSON MARRIAGE

This gentleman, four times mayor of Colchester was held in great esteem by his fellow men. Many major projects in Colchester were supported by Mr. Wilson Marriage, namely, the Town Hall, Castle Park, Public Library, Albert Hall, Art Gallery and Schools, one school in particular, 'Barrack Street School' was renamed 'Wilson Marriage School' after his death in 1932.

Wilson Marriage owned the East Mill in Colchester along with barges that conveyed his cargoes of grain to the mill for processing. A keen supporter of the Silver Band, he was much respected by the people of Alresford.

ALRESFORD GRANGE

This large building with its gracious gardens overlooking the river Colne was built in 1910 for Mr. Wilson Marriage. A prominent flour miller, Mr. Marriage owned barges that took his grain to the East Mill in Colchester, he also owned and farmed the nearby Marsh farm at Alresford.

Whilst sailing up the river Colne, Mr. Marriage a keen yachtsman spotted this lovely secluded site on a hill, he decided there and then that this was to be his new home.

Many local residents will have had close relatives who were employed by Mr. Marriage. His employees worked as gardeners, kitchen maids and housemaids. 'Being in Service' was the term used to describe a person working in this type of environment.

During the Second World War, Alresford Grange was taken over by the British Army. A number of troops from an Anti Tank Regiment were stationed here in 1941 to defend the East Anglian Coastline. Living conditions at the Grange was not good. Whilst the officers were housed in the Grange itself, the soldiers were obliged to sleep in bathing huts that were located within the grounds. There was no heating in these huts. During the cold winter months, soldiers slept in their clothing and boots to keep themselves warm. Many of these troops were regulars at the 'Pointer Inn' and the Village Hall.

According to one source, the people of Alresford made these soldiers very welcome indeed during their stay here.

ALRESFORD GRANGE

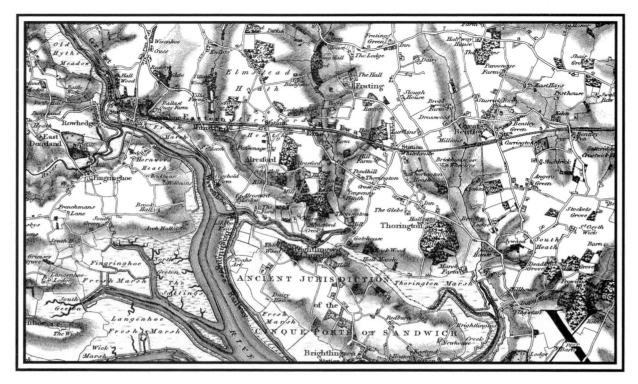

MAP OF ALRESFORD c.1860

This ancient map shows the estuary at the mouth of the river Colne as it wends its way past the town of Brightlingsea and the small village of Thorrington to the right of the river, whilst to the left of the river lies the villages of West and East Mersea, Langenhoe and Fingringhoe.

As the river meanders its way past Alresford, Rowhedge, Wivenhoe, and the industrial area of the Hythe, it reaches the Oldest Recorded Town of Colchester.

This map will be useful to those readers wishing to follow the route of this tour.